YOU DON'T KNOW BLACK PEOPLE

A GUIDE FOR REPUBLICANS ON ATTRACTING BLACK AMERICANS TO THE PARTY

By

RIAN ANDERS

Copyright © 2024

INTRODUCTION

Welcome to the ultimate crash course in bridging the gap between red and blue – a journey filled with laughter, learning, and maybe a few awkward handshakes along the way. In this epic tome, we're diving headfirst into the complex, colorful, and downright confusing world of Black culture, politics, and everything in between.

First, throw everything you think you know out the window. If you purchased this book, you obviously don't know Black people. It's okay, I know Black people and want to guide you on this trip to the dark side.

But before we embark on this wild ride, let's address the elephant in the room – yes, I'm talking about the title of this book. "You Don't Know Black People"? Seriously? Now, I know what you're thinking – isn't that a bit... presumptuous? And you're right. Because the truth is, nobody knows Black people better than Black people themselves. But fear not, my dear readers, for this book isn't about claiming to know it all – it's about embracing the unknown, challenging your assumptions, and opening your minds to new perspectives.

So, what's this book all about, you ask? Well, I'm glad you asked, because we're about to embark on a whirlwind adventure through the heart and soul of Black America – from the barbershops of Harlem to the BBQ joints of Memphis, and everywhere in between. Along the way, we'll explore the rich tapestry of Black Americans, the nuances of Black politics, and the secrets to winning over Black voters (spoiler alert: it involves a lot of fried chicken and a little thing called dap).

But this book isn't just for politicians and political junkies – it's for anyone who's ever felt a little lost, a little out of touch, or a little too comfortable in their own bubble. It's for anyone who's ever wondered what it would take to bridge the gap between red and blue, black, and white, and everything in between. It's for anyone who's ever dared to dream of a brighter, more inclusive future for all Americans – one handshake, one conversation, and one vote at a time.

So, buckle up, my babies because we're about to embark on the adventure of a lifetime. From breaking stereotypes and building bridges to finding common ground one BBQ at a time, get ready to laugh, learn, and maybe even dap your way to victory. Because

when it comes to winning over Black voters, a little
humor, humility, and heart go a long way.

So, cop a squat, grab a snack, and get ready to dive
headfirst into the wild and wonderful world of "You
Don't Know Black People: A Guide for Republicans on
Attracting Black Americans to the Party." Trust me,
folks – it's gonna be a ride you won't soon forget.

TABLE OF CONTENTS

LEGAL NOTES

The contents of this book are the sole expression of the author's thoughts and opinions and do not necessarily reflect those of Amazon Kindle Direct Publishing or any other parties associated with the publication of this book.

The author and publisher make no representations or warranties about the accuracy or completeness of the information contained in this book. The author and publisher assume no liability for any loss or damage caused by the use of the information contained in this book.

The contents of this book are for informational purposes only and should not be interpreted as professional advice. The author and publisher are not responsible for any actions taken as a result of reading this book.

Chapter 1. Breaking Stereotypes and Building Bridges

In the realm of politics, perceptions often overshadow realities. When it comes to engaging with Black Americans, the Republican Party faces a persistent challenge: understanding a diverse community beyond the confines of stereotypes. To attract Black voters, Republicans must embark on a journey of empathy, actively listening, and demonstrating genuine concern for the issues that matter most to this demographic.

It starts with acknowledging that the Black community is not a monolith. Within its ranks exist a multitude of perspectives, experiences, and aspirations. By recognizing this diversity, Republicans can begin to foster meaningful connections and dispel the notion that their party is inaccessible or indifferent to the concerns of Black Americans.

One of the first steps in bridging this gap is to engage in dialogue, not just during election cycles, but year-round. Listening sessions, town halls, and community forums provide invaluable opportunities to hear directly from Black constituents about their needs, hopes, and frustrations. By actively seeking input and feedback, Republicans can demonstrate a genuine commitment to understanding and addressing the issues that affect Black communities.

Moreover, it's essential to confront the historical and systemic barriers that have marginalized Black Americans for generations. From economic disparities to inequities in education and criminal justice, the legacy of racism continues to shape the lived experiences of millions of individuals across the country. Republicans must acknowledge this reality and advocate for policies that promote equality of opportunity and address the root causes of social injustice.

Additionally, representation matters. The Republican Party must actively recruit and support Black candidates at all levels of government. By elevating diverse voices within their ranks, Republicans can demonstrate their commitment to inclusion and broaden their appeal to Black voters.

Ultimately, attracting Black Americans to the Republican Party requires more than just rhetoric—it demands meaningful action. By challenging stereotypes, fostering dialogue, advocating for change, and embracing diversity, Republicans can begin to build trust and forge lasting connections with Black communities across the nation. As the adage goes, "You don't know Black people"—but with empathy, engagement, and a genuine commitment to change, Republicans have the opportunity to rewrite the narrative and build a more inclusive future for all Americans.

Chapter 2. Finding Common Ground, One BBQ at a Time

Alright, so you want to know how to win over Black voters to the Republican Party? Well, grab your apron and fire up the grill because we're about to embark on a journey of smoked meats, soulful tunes, and maybe a little bit of political persuasion.

First things first, let's talk about the importance of food. You see, food has a magical way of bringing people together—Democrats, Republicans, Independents, you name it. So, if you're trying to connect with Black voters, there's no better place to start than a good ol' backyard BBQ. Whip up some ribs, chicken, and all the fixings, and watch as the conversation starts flowing faster than the hot sauce.

Now, when it comes to music, you've got to get it right. Leave the country tunes at home and opt for some classic R&B or hip-hop jams. Trust me, nothing gets heads nodding and hips swaying like a little bit of Marvin Gaye or Beyoncé.

But enough about the ambiance—let's get down to business. When you're chatting with Black voters, it's important to keep it real. None of that rehearsed politician-speak, please. Instead, show some personality, crack a joke or two, and don't be afraid to laugh at yourself. After all, a little humor can go a long way in breaking down barriers and building genuine connections.

Oh, and speaking of humor, let's address the elephant in the room: yes, we're talking about race. But here's the thing—it doesn't have to be awkward. In fact, embracing diversity and celebrating different perspectives can make for some hilarious conversations. So, don't shy away from the tough topics—lean in, listen, and learn. Who knows, you might just find that you have more in common than you think.

In the end, winning over Black voters to the Republican Party is all about finding common ground, one BBQ at a time. So, fire up the grill, crank up the music, and get ready to make some new friends. After all, as they say, the quickest way to a voter's heart is through their stomach—and a side of good conversation doesn't hurt either.

CHAPTER 3. UNDERSTANDING THE POWER OF CULTURE

Let's jump into the colorful world of culture and why it's essential for bridging the gap between Republicans and Black Americans.

Now, I know what you're thinking – culture? Isn't that just fancy talk for hip-hop music and soul food? Well, yes and no. While those things are undeniably awesome, culture runs much deeper than a catchy beat or a plate of delicious ribs. FYI, Black people take food seriously.

First off, let's talk about the power of cultural appreciation. Imagine you're at a party, and someone compliments your taste in music. Instantly, you feel a connection – a sense of camaraderie that transcends political differences. That's the magic of cultural appreciation, my friends. By showing genuine interest in Black culture – whether it's through music, art, or cuisine – you're building bridges and creating common ground where none existed before.

But wait, there's more! Understanding the nuances of Black culture isn't just about scoring points at the next neighborhood cookout (although, let's be real, that's a tremendous bonus). It's about showing respect for the rich tapestry of experiences that make up the Black American identity.

So, how do you go about understanding Black culture without accidentally stepping on any cultural landmines? Well, for starters, put down the history books and pick up a conversation. Ask questions, listen attentively, and approach each interaction with an open mind and a willingness to learn.

Don't say idiotic things that cause Black X (formerly known as Twitter) to come together in unison to express their extreme disgust. All Black people do not like the same things, nor do they all live in the inner city. Again, speak to an actual Black American.

Next, don't be afraid to step outside your comfort zone and try new things. Whether it's attending a local jazz concert, exploring a Black-owned business in your community, or simply striking up a conversation with your Black neighbors, embrace the opportunity to immerse yourself in unfamiliar experiences. Who knows? You might just discover a newfound appreciation for Afrobeat music or a newfound love for collard greens.

Finally, remember that cultural understanding is an ongoing journey, not a destination. Keep an open heart and a curious mind as you continue to explore the rich diversity of Black culture. And who knows? Along the way, you might just find yourself forming genuine connections and building lasting friendships with Black Americans who share your values and aspirations.

Chapter 4. The Art of Authentic Outreach

Get ready for the delicate dance of authentic outreach—the secret sauce to winning over Black voters without breaking a sweat (or your bank account).

Now, I know what you're thinking – authentic outreach? Isn't that just a fancy way of saying "please like us"? Well, not quite. Authentic outreach is more than just a superficial attempt to win over Black voters – it's about building genuine connections and fostering trust through meaningful engagement.

So, how do you master the art of authentic outreach without coming across like a used car salesman at a family reunion? Fear not, my fellow Republicans – I've got you covered with a few handy tips and tricks:

Be Genuine: First things first, authenticity is key. Don't try to be something you're not or pretend to understand experiences you've never lived. Instead, approach each interaction with humility, honesty, and a genuine desire to learn from the perspectives of Black Americans.

Listen More, Talk Less: As tempting as it may be to launch into a passionate speech about tax reform or healthcare policy, sometimes the best approach is to simply listen. Take the time to hear the concerns, hopes, and aspirations of Black voters without interrupting or interjecting your own opinions.

Show Up, But Don't Show Off: When it comes to outreach events and community gatherings, it's important to show up and be present. But remember, this isn't your moment to shine – it's a chance to support and uplift Black voices. So, leave the campaign buttons and slogan-filled speeches at home and focus on building relationships instead.

Get Creative: Outreach doesn't have to be boring! Think outside the box and get creative with your engagement efforts. Host a neighborhood BBQ, organize a community clean-up event, or sponsor a local talent show – the possibilities are endless. Just make sure to keep the focus on building connections and fostering goodwill, rather than scoring political points.

Follow Up: Finally, don't forget to follow up! Building relationships takes time and effort, so be sure to stay in touch with the people you meet along the way. Send a thank-you note, invite them to future events, or simply check in to see how they're doing – small gestures can go a long way in building trust and goodwill.

CHAPTER 5. THE POWER OF REPRESENTATION

In this chapter, we're diving into the transformative power of representation – a.k.a. why seeing is believing when it comes to winning over Black voters.

Now, I know what you're thinking – representation? Isn't that just a buzzword thrown around by Hollywood types and social justice warriors? Well, not exactly. Representation is more than just a trendy hashtag – it's about seeing yourself reflected in the world around you, whether it's in politics, media, or everyday life.

So, why does representation matter in the context of attracting Black Americans to the Republican Party? It's simple, really. When Black voters see people who look like them in positions of power and influence within the party, it sends a powerful message – that their voices are heard, their concerns are valued, and their perspectives are respected.

But here's the catch – representation isn't just about optics. It's about meaningful action and genuine

commitment to diversity and inclusion. So how do
Republicans go about achieving meaningful
representation within the party? Let's break it down:

Walk the Walk: Talk is cheap, but actions speak
volumes. If Republicans want to attract Black voters,
they need to demonstrate a genuine commitment to
diversity and inclusion within the party. This means
actively recruiting and supporting Black candidates for
political office, appointing Black leaders to key
positions within the party, and advocating for policies
that uplift and empower Black communities.

Amplify Black Voices: Black Americans have a wealth
of knowledge, expertise, and lived experiences that
can enrich the Republican Party – if only they're given
the chance to be heard. Republicans should actively
seek out and amplify the voices of Black leaders,
activists, and community organizers, both within the
party and beyond. By elevating Black voices and
perspectives, Republicans can demonstrate their
commitment to inclusion and representation.

Build Bridges, Not Walls: Representation isn't just
about putting Black faces on campaign posters – it's
about building meaningful relationships and fostering

trust with Black communities. Republicans should prioritize outreach efforts that center on genuine engagement and dialogue, rather than token gestures or photo ops. Whether it's attending community events, hosting town hall meetings, or simply having conversations with Black voters, Republicans should be willing to roll up their sleeves and do the hard work of building bridges, one conversation at a time.

Embrace Diversity of Thought: Black Americans are not a monolithic group – we have diverse perspectives, beliefs, and ideologies, just like any other community. Republicans should embrace this diversity of thought and welcome Black Americans who may not fit neatly into traditional party lines. By creating a big tent that welcomes diverse perspectives and voices, Republicans can demonstrate their commitment to representation and inclusion.

Chapter 6. Bridging the Economic Divide

In this chapter, we're tackling one of the most critical issues facing Black Americans – the economic divide – and exploring how Republicans can bridge this gap to win over Black voters.

Now, I know what you're thinking – economics? Isn't that just a fancy way of saying "money stuff"? Well, yes and no. While economics certainly involves money, it's also about so much more – it's about opportunity, empowerment, and the pursuit of the American Dream. And for far too many Black Americans, the dream feels more like a distant mirage than a tangible reality.

So, how can Republicans address the economic challenges facing Black communities and earn their trust and support in the process? Let's dive in:

Economic Empowerment: The first step in bridging the economic divide is to empower Black Americans to achieve economic success and independence.

Republicans should champion policies that create opportunities for entrepreneurship, job creation, and wealth-building within Black communities. This means supporting small businesses, investing in workforce development programs, and removing barriers to economic mobility.

Education and Skills Training: Education is the great equalizer, but far too many Black Americans lack access to quality education and skills training opportunities. Republicans should advocate for policies that ensure every child has access to a high-quality education, regardless of their zip code. This means expanding school choice, investing in vocational training programs, and promoting STEM education initiatives that prepare students for success in the 21st-century economy.

Financial Literacy and Wealth Management: Knowledge is power, especially when it comes to personal finance. Republicans should prioritize financial literacy initiatives that equip Black Americans with the knowledge and skills they need to make informed financial decisions, build wealth, and achieve financial security. This means promoting financial education programs in schools, community centers, and churches, and providing resources and support to help Black families build a strong financial foundation.

Investing in Infrastructure: Infrastructure is the backbone of economic growth and prosperity, but far too many Black communities lack access to basic infrastructure like affordable housing, reliable transportation, and quality healthcare. Republicans should prioritize infrastructure investments that benefit underserved communities and create jobs and economic opportunities for Black Americans. This means investing in affordable housing initiatives, improving public transportation networks, and expanding access to healthcare services in underserved areas.

Criminal Justice Reform: The criminal justice system is a major barrier to economic opportunity for many Black Americans, with mass incarceration and systemic racism disproportionately impacting Black communities. Republicans should champion criminal justice reform efforts that address racial disparities in the criminal justice system, promote alternatives to incarceration, and support reentry programs that help formerly incarcerated individuals reintegrate into society and find employment.

By addressing the economic challenges facing Black
communities head-on and championing policies that
promote economic empowerment, opportunity, and
inclusion, Republicans can bridge the economic
divide and earn the trust and support of Black voters.
So, let's roll up our sleeves, get to work, and build a
brighter, more prosperous future for all Americans –
together.

CHAPTER 7. NAVIGATING THE CULTURAL LANDSCAPE

We're taking a humorous yet insightful look at navigating the cultural landscape – because let's face it, sometimes understanding Black culture can feel like trying to decipher hieroglyphics while riding a unicycle. But fear not, my fellow Republicans, for I'm here to guide you through the labyrinth of cultural nuances with wit, charm, and a healthy dose of self-awareness.

Now, I know what you're thinking – cultural landscape? Isn't that just a fancy way of saying "what the heck is going on"? Well, you're not entirely wrong. The cultural landscape is a complex tapestry of traditions, customs, and social norms that shape the way Black Americans interact with the world around them. And if you want to win over Black voters, you'll need to learn how to navigate this terrain with finesse and grace (or at least a good sense of humor).

So, let's dive into the cultural deep end and explore some of the key landmarks:

Music and Dance: Ah, music – the universal language that brings us all together, even if we can't agree on whether to call it hip-hop, rap, or just plain good old music. Black Americans have made immeasurable contributions to the world of music, from jazz and blues to gospel and R&B. So why not take a cue from our playlist and groove to the beat of Black culture? Who knows, you might just discover a newfound appreciation for the funky rhythms of James Brown or the soulful crooning of Aretha Franklin.

Food and Cuisine: They say the way to a person's heart is through their stomach, and nowhere is that truer than in the world of Black cuisine. From soul food staples like fried chicken and collard greens to Caribbean delicacies like jerk chicken and oxtail stew, Black Americans have perfected the art of comfort food. So why not expand your culinary horizons and sample some of the delicious flavors of Black culture? Just be sure to bring your appetite – you're gonna need it!

Art and Expression: Art comes in many forms, whether it's a powerful painting that captures the essence of the human experience or a thought-provoking poem that stirs the soul. Black Americans have a rich artistic heritage that spans centuries, from the Harlem Renaissance to the Black Lives Matter movement. So why not take a moment to appreciate the beauty and creativity of Black culture? Who knows, you might just find inspiration in the unlikeliest of places.

Language and Vernacular: Ain't nothin' like a good ol' fashioned Southern drawl to liven up a conversation, am I right? Black Americans have a unique way with words, whether it's slang, dialect, or just plain old colorful expressions. So why not embrace the linguistic quirks of Black culture and sprinkle a little flavor into your conversations? Just be sure to keep it respectful – nobody likes a cultural appropriator.

Celebrations and Traditions: From Juneteenth celebrations to Kwanzaa gatherings, Black Americans know how to throw a party – and you're invited! So why not join in the fun and experience the joy and camaraderie of Black culture firsthand? Whether you're dancing to the rhythm of the drum or feasting on traditional delicacies, you're sure to have a blast and make some unforgettable memories along the way.

CHAPTER 8. THE AWKWARD YET ESSENTIAL ART OF "DAP"

Get ready to delve into the delightful world of "dap" –
the handshake that's more than just a handshake, it's
a cultural phenomenon.

Now, I know what you're thinking – dap? Isn't that just
another word for "hello" or "what's up"? Well, my dear
Republican friends, dap is so much more than a mere
greeting. It's a complex dance of handshakes, fist
bumps, and intricate finger snaps that's as much
about style as it is about substance.

So, why should Republicans care about mastering the
art of dap? It's simple – dap is the universal language
of brotherhood and camaraderie in Black culture.
When done right, a well-executed dap can convey
respect, solidarity, and a sense of belonging that

transcends political differences. Plus, it's a surefire way to earn some serious street cred with Black voters.

But here's the catch – dap isn't something you can fake or force. It's a subtle yet essential part of Black culture that requires finesse, timing, and a good sense of rhythm. So, let's break it down, shall we?

The Fist Bump: Ah, the classic fist bump – a timeless gesture of solidarity and respect. When offering a fist bump, make sure to extend your fist with confidence and purpose, but be sure not to come on too strong – nobody likes a fist bump that feels more like a punch in the face.

The Snap and Slide: For the more advanced dap aficionados, the snap and slide is where it's at. Start by snapping your fingers in sync with your partner, then smoothly transition into a sliding motion that ends with a subtle finger point or fist tap. It's a move that screams "I'm cool, I'm hip, and I'm totally down with the culture."

The Handshake/Hug Combo: Sometimes, a simple handshake just won't cut it – you need something with a little more pizzazz. Enter the handshake/hug combo – a delightful fusion of two classic gestures that's equal parts formal and friendly. Just be sure to gauge your partner's comfort level before going in for the hug – nobody likes a surprise embrace.

The Elbow Bump: In these socially distant times, the elbow bump has become the go-to greeting for germaphobes and trendsetters alike. Simply extend your elbow towards your partner and lightly tap elbows in a show of mutual respect and solidarity. It's the perfect way to stay safe while keeping cool.

The Secret Handshake: Last but not least, the secret handshake – because who doesn't love a little mystery and intrigue? Whether it's a series of intricate hand movements or a top-secret code word, the secret handshake is the ultimate sign of camaraderie and belonging. Just make sure to keep it under wraps – after all, it's called a secret handshake for a reason.

Bam…there you have it, folks – Chapter 8 of "You Don't Know Black People: A Guide for Republicans on Attracting Black Americans to the Party." Stay tuned for more laughs, insights, and unexpected revelations as we continue our journey to bridge the gap and build a brighter, more inclusive future for all. And remember – when it comes to mastering the art of dap, practice makes perfect. Go get out there, shake some hands (or elbows), and show Black voters that you're ready to dap it up and get down to business!

Chapter 9. The Soulful Serenade of Southern Cuisine

Today, we're embarking on a culinary adventure through the soulful landscapes of Southern cuisine – a journey that promises to tantalize your taste buds, warm your heart, and maybe even win you some votes along the way.

Now, you might be wondering – why Southern cuisine? Isn't that just a fancy way of saying "fried chicken and sweet tea"? Well, my dear Republican friends, Southern cuisine is so much more than a simple meal – it's a celebration of history, heritage, and hospitality that's as rich and flavorful as a slice of homemade pecan pie.

So, grab your aprons and prepare to feast your eyes (and stomachs) on some of the most iconic dishes of the South:

Fried Chicken: Ah, fried chicken – the crown jewel of Southern cuisine and a beloved staple of backyard barbecues and Sunday dinners alike. Crispy on the outside, tender on the inside, and seasoned to perfection with a secret blend of herbs and spices, fried chicken is more than just a meal – it's a rite of passage for anyone seeking to win over the hearts (and stomachs) of Black voters.

Collard Greens: No Southern meal would be complete without a heaping pile of collard greens – a nutritious and delicious side dish that's as essential to the Southern culinary experience as grits and gravy. Slow-cooked with smoked ham hocks, onions, and garlic until tender and flavorful, collard greens are the epitome of comfort food – and a surefire way to earn some serious street cred with Black voters.

Macaroni and Cheese: Creamy, cheesy, and oh-so-indulgent, macaroni and cheese is a Southern classic that's guaranteed to put a smile on your face and a skip in your step. Whether baked to golden perfection or served up in a gooey, stovetop-style pot, mac and cheese is the ultimate comfort food – and a must-have addition to any Republican outreach event or campaign rally.

Sweet Potato Pie: Move over, pumpkin – there's a new pie in town, and it goes by the name of sweet potato. Rich, creamy, and packed with warm spices like cinnamon, nutmeg, and ginger, sweet potato pie is a Southern delicacy that's sure to delight your taste buds and win over even the most skeptical of voters. So go ahead, take a bite – and let the sweet, soulful flavors of the South transport you to a place where politics takes a back seat to good food and good company.

Peach Cobbler: C, we have peach cobbler – a quintessential Southern dessert that's as sweet as a summer breeze and as comforting as a warm hug. Made with fresh, juicy peaches and topped with a buttery, golden crust, peach cobbler is the perfect way to end any meal – and the perfect way to show Black voters that you're ready to embrace the rich culinary heritage of the South.

CHAPTER 10. THE GRAND FINALE: TURNING RED STATES BLUE... JEANS

Welcome, dear readers, to the grand finale of "You Don't Know Black People: A Guide for Republicans on Attracting Black Americans to the Party." We've laughed, we've learned, and we've probably eaten way too much fried chicken – but our journey is far from over. In this epic conclusion, we're pulling out all the stops and unveiling the ultimate secrets to turning red states blue... jeans. That's right, it's time to roll up our sleeves (and our pant legs) and get down to the serious business of winning over Black voters – one pair of denim-clad hips at a time.

Now, I know what you're thinking – jeans? Isn't that just a piece of clothing? Well, my dear Republican friends, jeans are more than just a fashion statement – they're a symbol of American culture, freedom, and rugged individualism. And if you want to win over Black voters, you'll need to learn how to speak their language – and that language just happens to be denim.

So, without further ado, let's dive into the denim-clad depths of Chapter 10:

The Power of the Blue Jean: Jeans are the great equalizer – the one piece of clothing that transcends age, race, and political affiliation. Whether you're a cowboy, a rock star, or a politician on the campaign trail, chances are you've got a pair of jeans hanging in your closet. So why not harness the power of the blue jeans to connect with Black voters on a deeper level? Throw on a pair of Levi's, roll up your sleeves, and show Black voters that you're just a regular Joe (or Jane) who's ready to listen, learn, and laugh.

Denim Diplomacy: Forget about fancy suits and power ties – when it comes to winning over Black voters, denim is the ultimate diplomatic tool. Whether you're knocking on doors, attending community events, or hosting a campaign rally, a well-worn pair of jeans can go a long way in breaking down barriers and building trust. So don't be afraid to embrace your inner cowboy (or cowgirl) and strut your stuff in a pair of jeans that says, "I'm one of you."

Dressing for Success: They say clothes make the man (or woman), and nowhere is that truer than in the world of politics. But forget about designer suits and expensive accessories – when it comes to winning over Black voters, less is more. Keep it simple, keep it casual, and let your personality shine through. After all, nothing says "I'm here to listen" like a pair of jeans and a genuine smile.

The Art of the Jean Jacket: If jeans are the bread, then jean jackets are the butter – a delightful addition to any political wardrobe that's sure to turn heads and win hearts. Whether you're rocking a classic Levi's trucker jacket, or a vintage find from the thrift store, a well-worn jean jacket is the perfect way to add a touch of Americana to your campaign look. So, throw on your favorite denim outerwear, channel your inner James Dean, and get ready to make a statement that's as timeless as it is stylish.

Making History in Denim: As we embark on this final chapter of our journey, let's remember that history is made not by those who play it safe, but by those who dare to be different. Embrace the power of denim, the spirit of inclusivity, and the promise of a brighter, more united future for all Americans. Together, we can turn red states blue... jeans.

And so, dear readers, we come to the end of our journey – a journey filled with laughter, learning, and maybe a few too many corny jokes. But as we bid farewell to "You Don't Know Black People: A Guide for Republicans on Attracting Black Americans to the Party," let's remember that the real work is just beginning. So, let's roll up our sleeves, slip into our favorite pair of jeans, and get ready to make history – one denim-clad vote at a time.

Conclusion

Conclusion: Dap, Denim, and the Road Ahead

Well, folks, we've reached the end of our wild ride through "You Don't Know Black People: A Guide for Republicans on Attracting Black Americans to the Party." And what a ride it's been – from breaking stereotypes and building bridges to finding common ground one BBQ at a time, we've laughed, we've learned, and we've probably eaten way too much fried chicken. But as we bid farewell to this epic journey, let's take a moment to reflect on all we've discovered along the way.

We've learned that representation matters, whether it's in politics, media, or the world of dap. We've learned that cultural appreciation is about more than just enjoying soul food and sweet tea – it's about understanding, respect, and genuine connection. And we've learned that when it comes to winning over Black voters, a little humor, humility, and denim go a long way.

So where do we go from here? Well, my dear Republican friends, the road ahead may be long and winding, but it's also filled with endless possibilities. As we embrace the power of dap, denim, and the democratic process, let's remember that change doesn't happen overnight – it happens one handshake, one conversation, and one vote at a time.

So, let's roll up our sleeves, slip into our favorite pair of jeans, and get ready to make history – because when it comes to building a brighter, more inclusive future for all Americans, there's no time like the present. So go forth, my fellow Republicans, and may the spirit of dap be with you as you embark on this grand adventure. And who knows? With a little humor, a lot of heart, and a whole lotta denim, anything is possible.

Until next time, keep dap'n, keep laugh'n, and keep fight'n the good fight. And remember – you don't know

Black people... until you do. Cheers, my friends, and
may the dap be with you!

About The Author

AUTHOR NAME is Rian Anders

Find out more at amazon.com/author/riananders